MAMMOTH

For a free color catalog describing Gareth Stevens Publishing's list of high-quality
books and multimedia programs, call 1-800-542-2595 (USA) or 1-800-461-9120 (Canada).
Gareth Stevens Publishing's Fax: (414) 225-0377.
See our catalog, too, on the World Wide Web: http://gsinc.com

Library of Congress Cataloging-in-Publication Data

Amery, Heather.
    Mammoth / by Heather Amery ; illustrated by Tony Gibbons.
       p. cm. — (The extinct species collection)
    Includes index.
    Summary: Describes the physical characteristics and habits of the prehistoric
ancestor of the elephant and discusses why it may have become extinct.
       ISBN 0-8368-1591-2 (lib. bdg.)
       1. Mammoth—Juvenile literature. [1. Mammoth. 2. Prehistoric animals.]
    I. Gibbons, Tony, ill. II. Title. III. Series.
    QE882.P8A45   1996
    569'.6—dc20   96-5000

First published in North America in 1996 by
Gareth Stevens Publishing
1555 North RiverCenter Drive, Suite 201
Milwaukee, Wisconsin 53212 USA

This U.S. edition © 1996 by Gareth Stevens, Inc. Created with original © 1995 by
Quartz Editorial Services, 112 Station Road, Edgware HA8 7AQ U.K., under the
title *Mammoths*.

Additional artwork by Clare Heronneau

U.S. Editors: Barbara J. Behm, Mary Dykstra

Printed in Mexico

1 2 3 4 5 6 7 8 9 9 99 98 97 96

MAMMOTH

Heather Amery
Illustrated by Tony Gibbons

Gareth Stevens Publishing
MILWAUKEE

Contents

Meet the mammoth

What an amazing sight **mammoths** must have been! They were huge prehistoric beasts, far bigger than today's elephants.

Mammoths lived long ago, when the climate was much colder than it is now. How did these huge animals find enough to eat in an icy environment? Are they all extinct, or could any of them still be alive? How do scientists know what **mammoths** looked like?

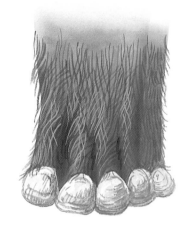

You'll find the answers to these questions and many more details about these enormous and fascinating creatures as you read.

These massive animals provided humans with food and clothing, as well as with materials for making tools.

Prehistoric

At first glance, it appears that **mammoths** looked much like today's elephants. Like elephants, they were herbivores, or plant-eaters. With their long trunks, **mammoths** would tear off grasses, flowers, moss, and leaves, as well as small branches from trees. They would then put the vegetation into their mouths and grind it up with teeth that were the size of bricks! When there was no food, they had to live off the fat stored in their bodies.

Herds of **mammoths** roamed Siberia, northern and eastern Europe, and North America from five million years ago until the end of the last Ice Age. They became extinct about ten thousand years ago.

Woolly mammoths, the best known of the **mammoth** family, had smaller ears than today's elephants, but larger tusks. The biggest **mammoth** tusk found was 13 feet (4 meters) long — about three times your height!

6

tusked beast

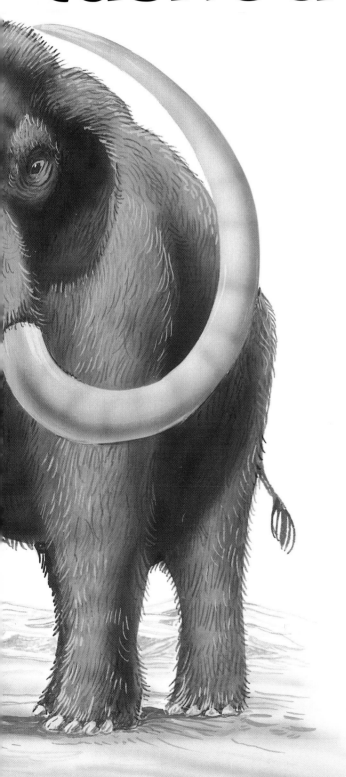

The **woolly mammoth** shown here was about 11.5 feet (3.5 m) tall. It weighed as much as eight large men would today. **Woolly mammoths** had shaggy coats of dark hair over thick woolen fur. Under their tough skin was a layer of fat that gave them added protection from the cold.

Like today's adult male elephants, adult male **mammoths** probably stayed by themselves, away from the rest of the herd.

About twenty-two months after mating, a female **mammoth** would give birth to one baby or, very rarely, twins. The babies were cared for by the mother, with the help of one or two other females in the herd, until they were about ten years old. Then they, too, were old enough to mate. A female had between five and fifteen young in her lifetime. The lifespan of a **mammoth** was probably about sixty to seventy years.

Life on the

The **woolly mammoth** was well suited to the times in which it lived. Conditions were cold and bleak throughout the Northern Hemisphere, with snow and ice covering much of the land. The **mammoth**'s thick, warm coat was ideal for protection against frigid temperatures.

Most of the **mammoth**'s time was spent looking for grass and other food. But vegetation was scarce due to the extreme climate. During the harshest weather, these huge creatures must have gone hungry.

Strange as it may seem, **mammoths** found it hard to adapt as the weather slowly warmed and the Ice Age drew to an end. They still inhabited colder areas, especially Siberia. But they no longer lived worldwide as their ancestors once had.

frozen lands

Self-defense

A small herd of **mammoths** lumbered slowly through the stunted trees, crunching the hard snow with their large, heavy feet.

When the leader raised her head and turned to look at a thick clump of bushes, the rest of the herd became nervous.

As they moved along, the leader — an elderly female — trumpeted.

She watched for a moment, then raised her trunk and trumpeted again.

She was calling to the other members of the herd to stay together. The others — females, young males, and babies — replied with growls and low rumbles, which came from deep within their throats.

This time it was an urgent call of alarm. She had caught sight of a pack of wolves, slowly creeping toward them. The wolves were hungry, drooling at the prospect of **mammoth** meat.

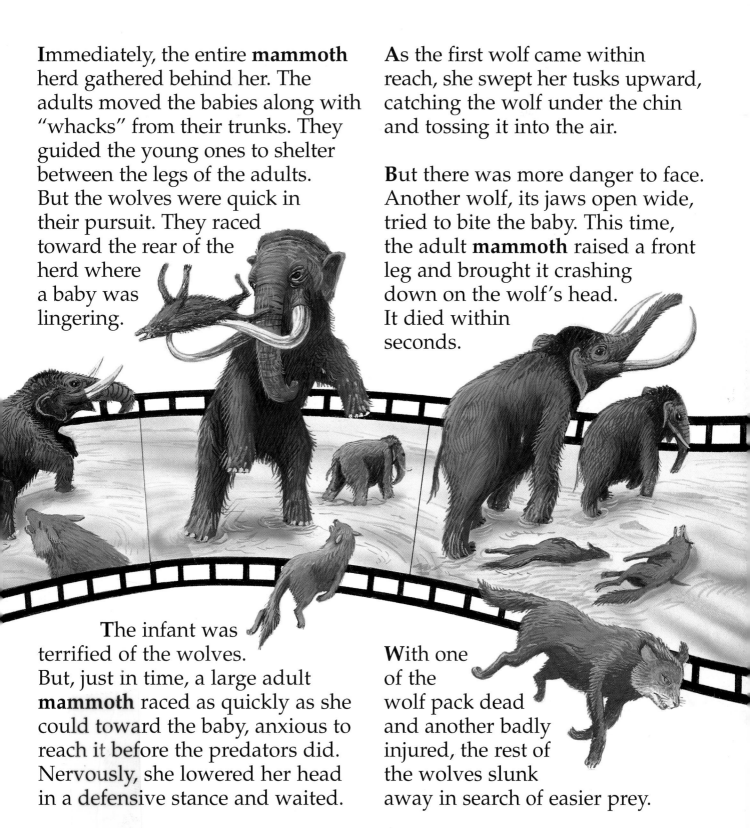

Immediately, the entire **mammoth** herd gathered behind her. The adults moved the babies along with "whacks" from their trunks. They guided the young ones to shelter between the legs of the adults. But the wolves were quick in their pursuit. They raced toward the rear of the herd where a baby was lingering.

As the first wolf came within reach, she swept her tusks upward, catching the wolf under the chin and tossing it into the air.

But there was more danger to face. Another wolf, its jaws open wide, tried to bite the baby. This time, the adult **mammoth** raised a front leg and brought it crashing down on the wolf's head. It died within seconds.

The infant was terrified of the wolves. But, just in time, a large adult **mammoth** raced as quickly as she could toward the baby, anxious to reach it before the predators did. Nervously, she lowered her head in a defensive stance and waited.

With one of the wolf pack dead and another badly injured, the rest of the wolves slunk away in search of easier prey.

11

Mammoth

The most important **mammoth** discoveries have been made in Siberia, where the remains of over 4,500 **mammoths** have been found. The frozen ground there has acted like a giant freezer, preserving the animals trapped in it.

One of the first Siberian discoveries was made in 1799 when an ice cliff thawed, slowly exposing the body of a **mammoth**. The carcass was eaten by dogs and wild animals, and the tusks were sold.

In 1900, the rotting body of a **mammoth** was found by a dog in Siberia. It appeared that the **mammoth** died when it fell off a cliff. Its body became exposed as the ground was eroded by wind and rain. Scientists concluded that it had been in the ground for about forty-five thousand years. Because its last meal was still in its stomach, scientists could even tell what foods it ate.

discoveries

This **mammoth**'s body was so well preserved that people even cooked and ate the meat of the animal.

More recently, a perfectly preserved baby **mammoth** was found frozen in the ground by a Siberian bulldozer operator. The animal was probably only six months old when it died. It perished forty thousand years ago after falling into a crevasse.

Remains of **mammoths** have been discovered in gravel and tar pits in many other parts of the world, such as North America, France, Germany, and Britain. However, none of the animals has been so well preserved as those found in Siberia.

The hunters

About fifty thousand years ago, during the last great Ice Age, groups of people known as Neanderthals lived in Europe and northern Asia. They were short and strong.

They hunted **mammoths** with wooden spears. They cooked the meat over fires and used the **mammoth** skins to keep warm. Neanderthals began to die out about forty thousand years ago.

They were gradually replaced by Cro-Magnon people. Cro-Magnons lived in caves or huts. They, too, hunted **mammoths** for food. They stored the meat in pits in the icy ground. Cro-Magnon humans also sewed **mammoth** skins together to make clothing. Cro-Magnons were cave artists. They drew the animals they saw and hunted on the walls of caves.

Cave paintings of **woolly mammoths** have been found in France, Germany, and Spain. These drawings have given scientists an excellent idea of what **mammoths** looked like.

15

Mammoth

Most scientists believe **mammoths** died out between 11,000 and 10,000 years ago. Some experts, however, think a few still could have been alive about 4,000 years ago.

Although it is not known for certain why **mammoths** became extinct, scientists do have several theories. Some scientists believe that toward the end of the last Ice Age — about 10,000 years ago — there may have been several severe cold spells. As a result, **mammoths** could not have found food and eventually would have starved to death.

As the weather gradually grew warmer, the ice began to melt. As the ground got softer, the heavy **mammoths** would have sunk into bogs, getting trapped in the mud and unable to escape. As the weather turned colder again, their bodies may then have frozen into the ground.

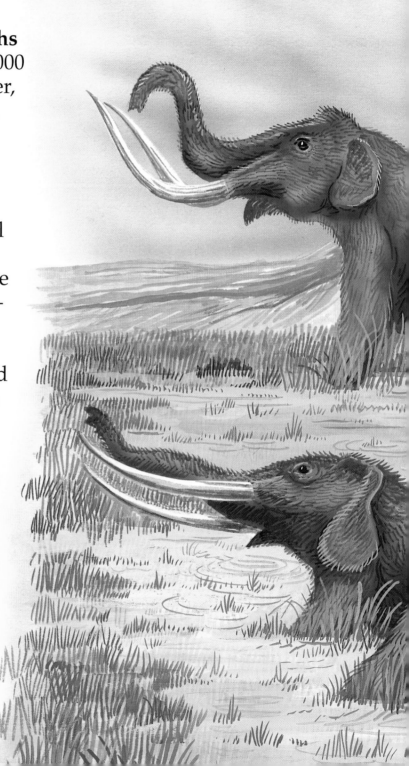

extinction

The remains of **mammoths** and other animals have been found in tar pits in places such as Rancho La Brea, California. The animals wandered into the water-filled pits and got stuck in tar beneath the water. Hunters might also have driven the animals into the pits.

Other scientists think **mammoths** may have run short of water. The animals may, therefore, have crowded around water holes, lakes, and rivers. The large numbers of **mammoths** in a small area may have depleted the nearby food supply.

As the **mammoths** gathered in increasing numbers, they may also have attracted large carnivores. Weak from lack of food and water, the **mammoths** would not have been able to fight off these aggressive, hungry predators. Disease may also have spread rapidly through such large herds, resulting in the deaths of many **mammoths**.

Surviving

Today, there are two kinds of elephants — the **African elephant**, known by scientists as *Loxodonta africana* (<u>LOCKS</u>-OH-<u>DON</u>-TAH <u>AF</u>-RICK-<u>AH</u>-NAH) (**1**), and the smaller **Indian elephant**, known as *Elephas maximus* (<u>EL</u>-EH-FAS <u>MAX</u>-IM-US) (**2**). Both are living relatives of the long-extinct **mammoth**.

Although they resemble **mammoths**, the two types of modern elephants are different from **mammoths** in several ways. Today's elephants are not as big as and do not have thick coats like the **woolly mammoths**. But elephants move in much the same way as their extinct cousins must have — plodding along on thick, sturdy legs. Elephants' tusks are not nearly as large as **mammoths**' were. And not all elephants have tusks. But both male and female **mammoths** had tusks. The males' tusks were thicker, heavier, and longer than the females'.

1

cousins

Today's elephants also have much larger ears, particularly the **African elephant**. It flaps them as a means of cooling off.

Today's elephants eat as much as 660 pounds (300 kilograms) of vegetation every day. But for the **mammoths**, there was far less plant life available in the frigid conditions. **Mammoths** often had to rely on stored body fat.

Elephants do not fully digest their food. Seeds from the food are distributed in the soil in elephant droppings. Perhaps **mammoths** also "planted" seeds in this manner.

An elephant's brain is small for its huge body, but it is over three times as heavy as a human brain. Experts believe elephants have a special means of communication that is too low in pitch for humans to hear. It is possible that **mammoths** had this system, as well.

2

A mammoth

There were several members in the **mammoth** family. All belonged to the same group of animals as today's elephants — *Proboscidea* (PROH-BOS-ID-EE-YA) — which means "long-snouted." Some experts think the word *mammoth* comes from the name *mam ntu*, or "earth mouse." This name was given to **mammoths** by the Tatars, a nomadic people who first found the animals' remains. Tatars believed these huge beasts lived underground.

The **woolly mammoth** — *Mammuthus primigenius* (MAM-OO-THUS PREE-ME-JEN-EE-US) **(1)** — is perhaps the best-known **mammoth**. Smaller than most of its North American cousins, it lived in Europe and Siberia. *Mammuthus trogontherii* (MAM-OO-THUS TROG-ON-THEAR-EE-EYE) **(2)**, also from central Europe, had huge tusks and a long, thick coat to protect it from cold temperatures. When temperatures became warmer, it retreated north.

1

2

gallery

Mammuthus imperator (MAM-<u>OO</u>-THUS IMP-<u>ER</u>-AH-<u>TOR</u>) (3), meanwhile, lived in North America. It was taller than today's giraffes, and its great tusks formed huge arcs. But there were smaller **mammoths**, too, such as *Mammuthus exilis* (MAM-<u>OO</u>-THUS <u>EX</u>-ILL-IS) (4).

A "pygmy" mammoth, *Mammuthus exilis* lived on islands off the coast of California. These islands were once part of the mainland. They formed when the sea level rose.

Some **mammoths** became trapped on these islands. Over generations, these animals gradually reduced in size because of a shortage of food. The *Moeritherium* (<u>MOW</u>-ER-EE-<u>THEAR</u>-EE-UM) (5), or dawn elephant, was also quite small. It did not have a trunk similar to a true **mammoth** or elephant, but it had front teeth that were like short tusks. Scientists think it is a distant ancestor not only of **mammoths**, but also of today's elephants.

3

4

5

Mammoth data

A mammoth needed a very strong skeleton to support its heavy body. It had a stiff, sloping backbone with large, strong legs. The legs were straight, like pillars, and not designed for speed. On each short, broad foot there were four short nails. A thick pad acted as a cushion under each foot.

Smaller females

Male **mammoths** were much bigger than the females. A fully grown adult male, for instance, could have been up to 3 feet (1 m) taller than a female and may have weighed up to twice as much. The males also had larger heads and longer, thicker tusks than females.

Turning around

A huge skull protected the **mammoth**'s brain and supported the weight of its enormous tusks. A **mammoth** could move its head up and down but could not turn it sideways. If a **mammoth** wanted to look backward, it had to turn around.

Sleeping habits

In spite of its large size, a **mammoth** could lie down to rest, slowly folding its legs and slumping onto the ground. It would sleep on the ground for several hours each night. It also napped, standing upright, during the day.

Ever-growing tusks

The **mammoth**'s long, curving tusks were actually two special teeth. These tusks grew slowly throughout a **mammoth**'s life. Although the tusks were not used as teeth, they still wore down at the tips. They could even be broken off during a fight.

Glossary

carnivore — a living being that eats only meat in order to survive.

crevasse — a deep crack in the ground, particularly in ice.

Cro-Magnons — early humans who lived at the same time and also after the time of Neanderthal humans. *Cro-Magnons* were named after a cave in France where their remains were first found.

herbivore — an animal that eats only vegetation, such as grass and other plants, in order to survive.

Ice Age — a period of time between 1.5 million and 10,000 years ago, when much of Earth was covered in snow and ice.

Neanderthal — a type of early human.

Proboscidea — the scientific name of a group to which mammoths and elephants, with their trunks and tusks, belong.

pygmy — any small object or person.

Rancho La Brea — a region in California that is now part of downtown Los Angeles. A great many prehistoric animals, including mammoths, became stuck in a tar pit there.

Siberia — a large region of northeast Asia, known for its extremely harsh winters.

Tatars — a nomadic people of Asia.

Index